BIRD ALERT

PEGGY THOMAS

BIRD ALERT

The Science of Saving Animals

TWENTY-FIRST CENTURY BOOKS
BROOKFIELD, CONNECTICUT

FOR HOWARD FACKLAM

THANKS DAD!

Acknowledgments
I would like to thank all the people who shared their expertise and enthusiasm with me, especially: Ward Stone, Chief Pathologist for NYSDEC; Sonny Knowlton, Wildlife Technician at the Iroquois Wildlife Refuge; Gavin Shire, former Chief Biologist at Airlie Enviromental Studies; Joseph Kuhn at the Keauhou Bird Conservation Center; and Rebecca Cann at the University of Hawaii.

Cover photography courtesy of © Joel Bennett/Peter Arnold, Inc.
Photographs courtesy of Animals Animals: pp. 2, 4, 11 (© Philip Hart), 33 (© M. Birkhead, OSF), 49 (© Johnny Johnson); The National Audubon Society Collection/Photo Researchers: pp. 6 (© G. C. Kelley), 15 (© C. O. Harris), 16 (left © John Mitchell), 43 (© Kenneth W. Fink), 55 (© Dyer); VIREO: p. 9 (© O. S. Pettingill, Jr.); U. S. Fish and Wildlife Service: p. 16 (right); © David Anderson, Wake Forest University: p. 18; © New York State Department of Environmental Conservation: p. 20; Peter Arnold, Inc.: p. 21 (© Thomas D. Mangelsen); Peggy Thomas: pp. 24, 26; Sharon Tiburzi: p. 27 (both); New York State Department of Environmental Conservation/Wildlife Pathology Unit: p. 31 (both); © Dr. Rebecca Cann: p. 36; © 1999 Zoological Society of San Diego: p. 38; © Jack Jeffrey: pp. 41, 44, 46; © Jim Denny: p. 45; © Gavin G. Shire: p. 50

Library of Congress Cataloging-in-Publication Data
Thomas, Peggy.
Bird alert / Peggy Thomas.
p. cm. — (The Science of saving animals)
Includes bibliographical references (p.).
Summary: Surveys programs and individuals dedicated to preserving birds and bird habitats.
ISBN 0-7613-1457-1 (lib. bdg.)
1. Birds—Juvenile literature. 2. Wildlife conservation—Juvenile literature.
[1. Birds. 2. Wildlife conservation.] I. Title.
QL676.2 T56 2000
333.95'8—dc21   00-025028

Published by Twenty-First Century Books
A Division of The Millbrook Press, Inc.
2 Old New Milford Road
Brookfield, Connecticut 06804
www.millbrookpress.com

CONTENTS

A male rufous hummingbird hovers before moving on to the next flower.

1 FOR THE BIRDS

Imagine looking up to see a flock of passenger pigeons so large and thick that it darkens the sky. You could have seen such a sight if you lived in the early 1800s. Back then, New York's state bird, the bluebird, would have been a fairly common sight, and in the Midwest, the sounds of migrating whooping cranes would have filled the air.

A lot has changed in two hundred years. It seems like a long time to us, but it's a brief blip in the life of a species. In that short time period, the bluebird became a rare sight in New York State, the number of whooping cranes in captivity outnumber their wild counterparts, and the passenger pigeon became extinct.

What will happen in the next two hundred years? The fate of many birds may depend on us.

FEATHERED FRIENDS

There are about 9,000 species of birds in the world, and no matter what they look like, everyone can tell that a bird is a bird. But birds are as different as the habitats they live in. They range in size from a delicate hummingbird that weighs as little as a stick of chewing gum, to a towering 200-pound (90-kilogram) ostrich. The streamlined arctic tern flies thousands of miles each year, while the stubby-winged New Zealand kiwi never gets off the ground. There are birds that dress in brilliant colors with plumes and fans for decoration, like the scarlet tanager or the Guatemalan quetzal, while others wear formal black and white like the tuxedoed penguins.

MAKING CONNECTIONS

Bird species survive in the coldest Antarctic waters, the most desolate deserts, and even the busiest cities. Their natural habitats helped define their behaviors and influenced their physical characteristics. In turn, birds play significant roles in the ecosystems they inhabit. For example, woodpeckers are house builders, drilling homes for other animals.

Every habitat also has its farmers. Hummingbirds and other pollen eaters pollinate flowers, while parrots, chickadees, and other seed- and fruit-eaters spread seeds. Some plants will only propagate when its seed goes through the digestive system of a specific species of bird. Birds are instrumental in keeping trees healthy by eating bugs that destroy leaves and spread disease. One study showed that trees completely covered with netting, which allowed insects in, but kept birds out, had twice as many insects and twice as much insect damage than trees left uncovered.

Raptors, or birds of prey, such as eagles, hawks, falcons, and owls, are in charge of pest control. They help keep the rodent population from exploding. At the top of the food chain, raptors are important environmental indicators, reflecting the health of the surrounding habitat. For example, the sudden decline of the peregrine falcon and the bald eagle in the 1960s warned scientists of the dangers of a pesticide called DDT. Today, yearly bird counts and complex computer models show scientists the rise and fall of bird species and point to changes in the environment that not only affect birds but people as well.

Kiwis have their nostrils at the tip of their bill and use their sense of smell to find food. They aren't usually seen during the day.

The more scientists learn about birds, the more they realize just how complex the connections are between birds, the environment, and other animals in the habitat. The disappearance of a bird species may cause problems that haven't even been considered yet.

HAZARDOUS HABITATS

Scientists are concerned about the health of bird species because birds are living in increasingly hazardous habitats, and unfortunately, most of the hazards are man-made: pesticides and other pollutants, fragmented forests, drained wetlands, and the spread of human developments.

The most immediate threat to bird survival is loss of habitat. Smaller forests don't just diminish the food supply or mean fewer trees to nest in. It alters the entire ecosystem, allowing new competitors and predators into the area. For example, migrating songbirds, called passerine species, prefer to live in the protected centers of undisturbed forests. Logging or fragmenting large tracts of forest creates smaller pockets of woods with more exposed edges. Predators such as raccoons, opossums, cats, and crows make their home at the forest's edge, raiding nests and eating young birds. In a Point Reyes Bird Observatory Newsletter, researcher Richard Stallcup calculated that there were roughly 44 million pet cats on the loose. If just one cat out of every ten killed one bird daily, that would add up to 4.4 million dead birds a day.

An altered forest environment also favors more adaptable birds like the cowbird, which practices nest, or brood, parasitism. Female cowbirds lay their eggs in the nests of other birds. Not knowing any better, the nesting parents take care of the larger cowbird chick at the expense of their own chicks, which usually do not survive. Some regions have been harder hit by the cowbird problem than others. Studies in Illinois have shown that at one time wood thrushes were basically raising nothing but cowbird chicks, whereas in Washington only 10 percent of nests were parasitized.

Although some birds can adapt to new habitats, many cannot survive the changes in diet, nesting sites, and enemies. Migratory birds are twice as vulnerable, because they rely on two habitats. Songbirds and raptors spend the winter in Central and South American countries, where the clear-cutting of forests continues at a fast pace, and the use of U.S.-banned pesticides continues.

And it is not uncommon for a population of migrating birds to travel south for the winter only to return north to an altered landscape the following spring. People have become expert in turning grasslands into farm fields and draining wetlands to create subdivisions and cities. More than half of the wetlands in the United States have already been drained and converted to communities and crisscrossed by roads. According to the Everglades National Park, so much of the water has been drained from the "river of grass" that the number of wading birds nesting there has declined by 90 percent since the 1930s.

Native species of North American birds have also been shoved out of their habitats, or killed by exotic invaders that have adapted

A lone snowy egret near Naples, Florida, is a sad remnant of the hundreds of thousands of birds that used to nest in southern Florida.

well to their new homes. For example, European starlings, English house sparrows, and pigeons brought to the United States compete for nesting sites and food with native wrens, chickadees, and bluebirds. People also brought predators such as dogs, mongooses, and cats to island habitats where native birds had no defense. Even exotic plants that become established in a natural habitat reduce the numbers of native plants that birds feed on.

Any form of pollution—air, water, noise, and even excessive light—can make a habitat unlivable for sensitive species. Oil from tanker spills damages the plumage of waterbirds and makes shorelines unfit for nesting sites. The light from city buildings and streets confuses birds that are migrating over urban areas, causing an estimated 100 million birds to crash into skyscrapers.

Pesticides, which are chemicals used to kill weeds, insects, and other pest animals, have also killed millions of birds. The Smithsonian Migratory Bird Center reports that throughout the world more than 5 billion pounds (2 billion kilograms) of pesticides are used each year. Twenty percent, or 1.2 billion pounds, is used in the United States alone. It's estimated that of the roughly 672 million birds exposed to pesticides in the United States each year, 10 percent, or 67 million, are killed. But it's difficult to know exactly how many birds die because most of the deaths go undetected.

All of these hazards come on the back of centuries of hunting birds for food, sport, and plumage. In the nineteenth century feathers were the fashion, and as many as 5 million beautiful birds were killed each year solely to produce fancy hats for women.

How do we keep the diversity of bird species for people to enjoy two hundred years from now? By learning as much as we can about the lives of birds, what they need to survive, and how they cope with the many stresses that humans place on their environments.

TEAM EFFORT

Ornithologists (scientists who study birds) are not alone in asking and answering questions about bird survival. It takes a team effort to study the complex problems of changing environments, pollution, and habitat loss. Different types of scientists look at bird survival in different ways. Some track bird migrations across hundreds of miles of open ocean, while others explore the insides of the living cell. Some study the dead, while others concentrate on producing future generations of birds. Many conservationists are just ordinary people who care. To be successful everyone must protect nesting sites, stop the use of deadly pesticides, help endangered birds reproduce, and most important, protect their habitats so we can keep birds flying free.

Math for Bird Brains

How do scientists know which birds are in most need of conservation help? They do the math. Each year the National Audubon Society puts out a WatchList of the birds that are most at risk. These birds are not on the endangered species list yet, with some help, they won't be.

Each species is graded on six criteria: how abundant they are, breeding distribution, conservation threats during breeding season, threats during nonbreeding season, and population trends. Each criteria is scored from 1 to 5. Five means a high risk, and one indicates a low risk. The scores are added, and those birds with the highest number need the most help. The plentiful robin, for example, has a score of 6, while the endangered whooping crane has a score of 30.

2 KEEP YOUR EYE ON THE BIRDIE

Birds can fly, but biologists can't. That's one fact of life that makes studying birds difficult. A scientist can have binoculars focused on a bird, then in an instant the bird flies from view. Perhaps it has just flown to another tree, but maybe it's started the first leg of a 1,000-mile (1,600-kilometer) migration. How do field biologists keep an eye on their study animal? They rely on high-tech equipment such as radio, video, and satellite technology. The first step in using some of this technology is catching the bird.

Small birds can be caught in a mist net made of thread so thin it is nearly invisible to a fast flier. A net is strung across an area more than 40 feet (12 meters) long and about 10 feet (3 meters) high. It looks like a delicate tennis net stretched taut with several tiers of loosely folded pockets. When a bird flies into the net, it falls into a pocket unharmed.

Raptors are lured out of the sky by a pigeon or other prey that is tethered to the ground. When the bird

A northern harrier is recovered from a bow net.

swoops in for the kill, it grabs the bait, triggering the net mechanism. The net snaps up and over the raptor, snaring the bird with the bait.

The nets are watched closely by researchers, who quickly and carefully untangle the birds. It is less stressful for a bird if it can't see what is happening, so its head is covered. Sometimes the bird is put into a cloth sack or a tube while it is waiting to be measured and banded.

BIRD BANDING

After a bird is taken from the net, its measurements are recorded along with the location and date. Then a small strip of aluminum, embossed with a number, is clamped loosely onto the bird's right leg. The bird is immediately released.

Scientists band about a million birds each year in the United States and Canada, hoping that some of them will be recaptured.

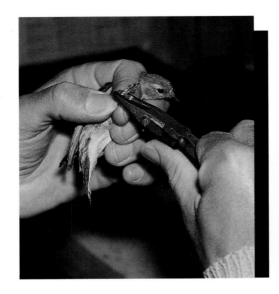

Banding a migrating goldfinch is delicate work.

Another successful banding at the Bird Banding Laboratory—a wood duck

Recording banded birds shows scientists where the birds go, how fast they travel, whether they keep the same mates, how long they live, and how they die. But only about 1 percent of the banded birds are ever recovered, either found dead or recaptured in another mist net.

All the bird-banding records are kept at the Bird Banding Laboratory in Laurel, Maryland. If you find a banded bird, you should call the lab at 1-800-327-BAND and report it. You will be told where, when, and why the bird was banded, and you'll be helping scientists learn a little more about that species.

RADIO RESEARCH

Although bird banding has provided scientists with many answers to bird behavior, scientists have even more questions to ask, such as finding out how birds use their habitat. Scientists follow birds using telemetry, or radio tracking. A bird is fitted with a small

Backpacks and Super Glue

Transmitters come in all shapes and sizes depending on the size of the bird and the length of time it will be tracked. The longer the time period, the larger, or stronger, the battery needs to be. Transmitters are attached in many ways. Some birds are fitted with backpacks that fit around each wing, but if a backpack unit isn't put on just right, the bird can walk right out of it. Other transmitters are attached with a leg band, or stuck on with a dab of super glue between the wings, or on the bird's tail feathers. Very small transmitters can be surgically implanted just under the skin on the back of the neck, or inside the chest cavity. The birds are put under anesthetic and the procedure takes no more than four minutes. After this minor surgery the birds are monitored a short time until they are well enough to be released.

radio transmitter before it is released to go about its normal activities. The transmitter is a high-tech mini radio that plays only one tune, a beep, beep sent out on the airwaves at a unique frequency. The only people who can hear the tune are field biologists with their receivers set at the same frequency.

To locate a bird, researchers use a handheld receiver with a directional antenna that looks like the letter H lying flat. For more distant locations or difficult terrain they also fly in an airplane equipped with antenna on each wing strut. When a signal is located, the researchers close in until the exact location is found and plotted on a map. Plotting the bird's movements shows scientists how birds use a habitat, how large an area they need, and where they nest—important information to have when developing conservation plans and judging the fitness of a species.

SIGNALS FROM SPACE

Radio transmitters carry signals several miles, but that's only a fraction of the distance flown each year by marathon migrators like arctic terns and whooping cranes or albatross that routinely fly

David Anderson (right) writes albatross data into a computer.

thousands of miles out at sea. For these long-distance fliers, researchers turn to satellite technology to keep in touch.

A satellite transmitter, the size of a Pez candy dispenser, is attached to the bird, where it sends out a signal that is picked up by one of several satellites that orbit Earth. The satellite notes the strength of the signal and its location, then transmits the information to one of three receiving stations on the ground. Scientists can keep track of their birds from just about anywhere on Earth as long as they have a computer terminal.

You can even track albatross on the Internet! David Anderson, a biologist at Wake Forest University, has posted information gathered from tracking two species of albatross as they travel from their

Albatross (Diomedeidae)

There are twenty-four species of albatross, stocky oceanic birds with a 12-foot (4-meter) wingspan, webbed feet, and hooked beak. The birds studied on Tern Island were Laysan and black-footed albatross. Albatross primarily live at sea, feeding on squid and fish, and come to shore only at nesting time. The birds lay one egg that is cared for by both parents until the chick is ready to fly. The oldest albatross recorded is sixty-six years old and is still alive.

nests on Tern Island near Hawaii. Albatross are ocean birds that feed on squid and fish far out at sea. They come to shore only to nest. No one knows how far they must travel to find enough food for themselves and their chicks, but it's important to find out because the birds are being caught accidentally by fishing fleets.

Many albatross populations are in decline as a result of long-line fishing, in which boats set out lines that are more than 60 miles (100 kilometers) long with 20,000 hooks attached. Some experts estimate as many as 10 billion hooks are set each year, and each one can potentially catch a bird. Albatross are attracted to the bait as the hooks are released behind a moving boat. When the bird attempts to steal the bait it gets hooked, pulled underwater, and drowns. Anderson hopes that tracking the Tern Island albatross will show scientists where the birds like to feed so that these areas can be protected from long-line and other dangerous fishing practices.

The albatross's enormous wingspan makes it well equipped for long journeys, but scientists never thought that nesting birds would fly so far from their young. "We seriously considered the possibility that the first bird had somehow gotten on a boat," Anderson said of one of his tracked albatross. The bird flew from Hawaii to San Francisco Bay and back, a weeklong oceanic flight of more than 5,000 miles (8,000 kilometers)! Scientists believe that the albatross may be going to the Pacific Coast of California for the rich food supply, which the birds digest and feed to its young. Now for the first time scientists have made the connection between the decline of the Tern Island albatross population with its possible cause—the long-line fishing that occurs off the Pacific Coast—and conservation measures can be taken.

CANDID CAMERA

A nest 70 feet (20 meters) off the ground is usually a private place, but not at the Iroquois National Wildlife Refuge in western New York. The bald eagles that nest there are being watched by thousands of visitors on television. Wildlife technician Sonny Knowlton and his crew attached video cameras to the eagle's basswood tree, allowing biologists to watch for the first time what goes on in an eagle's nest.

In addition to supervising video surveillance of the eagle's nest, Sonny Knowlton also bands birds. He's holding a juvenile osprey that will be banded— note the length of the talons.

This method of observation is called noninvasive, which means it doesn't disturb the birds or change the way they would normally behave. Nearly 20,000 people come each year to watch TV and see the male and female sit on their eggs, feed their young, or witness the eaglets' first flight.

The camera is set up each winter while the eagles are wintering down south. It must be in place by the end of January, before the eagles return in early February. "They will accept the equipment as normal as long as it's there before they arrive," Knowlton said. "Once it's up and

An impressive bald eagle makes a landing along the Alaskan coast.

Bald Eagle (*Haliaeetus leucocephalus*)

In the 1960s the bald eagle was in danger of becoming extinct throughout most of its range due to pesticides, hunting, and loss of habitat. But it has made a tremendous comeback. In the 1960s there were fewer than 450 bald eagle pairs in the Lower 48 states, but their numbers have soared to more than 5,000 pairs. Bald eagles get their trademark white head and tail feathers at four to five years. They live as long as thirty years. Eagles mate for life, and build giant nests that can reach 10 feet (3 meters) across and weigh as much as 2,000 pounds (900 kilograms). Bald eagles eat primarily fish, but will also hunt other small mammals and birds.

the eagles return, we don't touch it." The camera, which runs on solar panels and 12-volt batteries, sends a microwave signal that creates an image displayed on the television inside the visitor center.

"I have the ultimate couch potato job," Knowlton says. Part of his job may be to sit around and watch TV, but he has learned many things about eagle behavior that were not known before. He discovered that eagles continue to build their 6-foot (2-meter)-wide nest throughout their nesting season, right up until the eaglets leave the nest. He also found that eagles, which are predominantly fish eaters, will also eat many kinds of mammals, such as meadow voles.

Cameras have been focused on other birds' nests as well. The Microcam II, which has a lens the size of a dime, is surrounded by tiny infrared lights. It can film at night, and has recorded an army of fire ants attacking a nest of young black-capped vireos, which is one of the most endangered songbirds in the country. Without the cameras, the fire-ant problem might have gone unnoticed, but now other vireo nests can be protected.

3 CITIZEN SCIENCE

With a cup of coffee in one hand and a pencil in the other, Howard Facklam, a retired biology teacher, stares out the window and collects scientific data without ever leaving the comfort of his favorite chair. A hundred miles away, a group of fifth graders stare out their classroom window. Their teacher, Mrs. Doris Waud, doesn't mind as long as they're staring at birds.

The students and Mr. Facklam are just a few of the thousands of people who collect bird information for the Cornell Laboratory of Ornithology. "They call it 'citizen science,'" Mr. Facklam said. "because I'm not a professional scientist, but I love birds." As a member of the lab's Project FeederWatch, Facklam is recording data that will be used by researchers to create conservation plans for many bird species.

Ornithology is one of the few sciences in which amateurs play an important role, making discoveries and recording data. One of the oldest volunteer bird projects

Howard Facklam filling his feeders. The fat cylinder on the feeder pole keeps squirrels from eating the birdseed.

is the annual Christmas Bird Count run each year by the National Audubon Society. In 1900, twenty-seven conservationists started the Bird Count to protest the gruesome annual "side hunt," in which hunters competed against each other to see who could shoot the most birds on Christmas Day.

A hundred years later, Audubon's nationwide Christmas Bird Count involves more than 45,000 volunteers who go out and count all the bird species they see in one day. The Christmas Bird Count revolutionized bird studies, just as citizen science is changing the course of bird research today. It's speeding things up. In the 1980s, scientists realized that in order to develop conservation plans for declining bird populations, or just to identify those species that need help, they had to work fast. But the first step for any sound conservation plan is to know how many birds are out there, where they are, and how their numbers vary from year to year. Left to scientists alone, gathering such a large amount of data would take decades, but an army of volunteers can do it in much less time.

PROJECT FEEDERWATCH

There are several projects that bird buffs can volunteer for, and one of the largest is Project FeederWatch, in which people count the number of birds at their feeder during a specific observation time. In the winter of 1997–1998, more than 13,000 FeederWatchers— many of them kids—helped document bird populations.

Fifth graders at Fyle Elementary in Rochester, New York, watch the school's bird feeder for fifteen minutes during their designated days throughout November and March. At lunchtime they fill the feeders too. Kids who don't know a cardinal from a chickadee quickly learn how to identify them, as well as downy woodpeckers, house sparrows, and goldfinches. "They don't think they're doing science, but they are," said Mrs. Waud. "Not all science is whiz-bang discovery. Most of it is observing and taking notes."

The notes that FeederWatchers take—the temperature, precipitation, and number and type of birds—are recorded on bubble forms similar to those used in standardized tests in school. At the lab, the forms are checked for errors and put through an optical scanner that can process about 2,500 forms in one hour. But sending the information to the lab via the Internet is even faster. The data are immediately analyzed, creating up-to-the-minute accuracy about the number and location of birds.

Ten years of data really add up, and scientists have learned some interesting things they hadn't known before. They discovered that the dark-eyed junco, a type of finch, is the most widespread bird found at feeders in North America, and that it's normal for some birds to be abundant one winter and absent another. Trends over time show normal fluctuations in bird populations, but can also pinpoint significant declines that indicate a serious problem.

In 1993, for example, a disease caused by a bacteria thought to infect only poultry was found to cause eye infections in house finches. FeederWatchers were asked to record every sighting of dis-

(Left to right) Rebecca Burgio, Charlene Ward, and Lisa Palmieri
are three of the students at Fyle School in Rochester, New York,
involved in Project FeederWatch.

eased birds, which has helped track the spread of the infection
from Maryland, where it started, to every state east of the
Mississippi.

But you don't have to be enrolled in Project FeederWatch to
help birds. Some bird watchers go wild during spring and fall migration helping scientists count birds as they fly over the Cape May
Bird Observatory and other prime birding sites. Volunteers even
gather in New York City's Central Park to record the number of
hawks they can spot high in the sky as the birds pass over the city's
skyscrapers.

Some people come to the rescue when tragedy strikes, moni-
toring beaches and gathering injured shorebirds after oil spills.
Volunteers scrub gulls, terns, and even penguins to clean the thick
sticky oil from the birds' feathers.

ER FOR OWLS

When Sharon Tiburzi received her first injured owl, she was as afraid of the owl as it was of her. But after eight years of rehabilitation work, Tiburzi has become a specialist in taking care of these mysterious raptors of the night.

A wildlife rehabilitator is someone who is trained to handle and treat wild animals. Not just anyone can be a rehabilitator; you have to pass a test to earn a license.

But many rehab centers do need volunteers to help with the heavy workload. Everyday, bird cages must be cleaned, frozen mice thawed, birds fed, mouse cages cleaned, mice fed, birds exercised, and wounds treated. Rehabilitators agree that all the hard work is

At left is a barred owl that was hit by a car, leaving it blind in one eye with a broken wing; at right is an eastern screech owl also hit by a car. These are just two of the many owls Sharon Tiburzi has rescued and rehabilitated. The owls cannot be released to the wild, but they make many classroom visits and let people see for themselves how special owls are.

worth the thrilling moment when a healthy animal is released back into the wild.

It's a labor of love. Tiburzi volunteers her time, money, and effort to learn all she can about bird biology, nutrition, and basic veterinary care, and has turned her home into an owl haven. She has treated and released screech owls, great horned owls, and barn owls, as well as taken care of owls that can never be returned to the wild.

Tiburzi specializes in owls, in part, because they are so misunderstood. Each time she takes an owl out to a school or nature center she takes some of the audience's fear away by teaching the importance of owls in the environment, and how they are threatened by some of the things people do.

In thirty-five years of working with owls, Katherine McKeever of Ontario, Canada, figures that 85 percent of the injured small owls she treated had been hit by cars.

Owls are attracted to the roadside by the mice that live in the ditches, and feed on the garbage that people throw out of car windows. An owl will sit on a lamppost all night listening for the skittering of a mouse, then swoop down to grab its prey. The owl, however, is too focused on the hunt to be able to swerve out of the way of an oncoming car.

McKeever is convinced that litter-free roads would mean fewer injured owls. Owls would hunt elsewhere for food. One simple way ordinary citizens can help birds is to keep our roadsides clean.

4 THE BOD SQUAD

On any given day, Ward Stone might get a visit from a concerned citizen who has found a deformed deer, respond to a call about a rabid raccoon, or open a package containing several dead birds. It's all part of his job as the chief wildlife pathologist for New York State's Department of Environmental Conservation. A pathologist is a scientist who studies and monitors disease and causes of death. Every police department and hospital depends upon a good pathologist, but wildlife pathologists are rare. Very few state agencies have one.

"Some people think it's not very relevant to worry about an animal after it's dead," Stone said. "The real heroes are the ones that save the living. But if you can find out how a group of animals died, you can save millions of animals' lives."

And that's just what Stone and his staff do in their offices in Delmar, New York. Sick, injured, and dead animals are sent from all over the state. About one third of the cases involve birds. Stone's top priority are cases that pose a health hazard to people (such as rabies), involve hunting out of season, the illegal use of poisons, or anything that affects a large number of victims. He once investigated the death of 5,000 birds from thirteen species that were all found in one farmer's field, victims of pesticide poisoning.

A pathologist is like a detective who solves a murder. Both look for the murder weapon. Was it a gun, poison, or a car? Where did the deadly encounter happen, and is there a suspect? And most important, can other deaths be prevented in the future?

"Sometimes it takes a matter of seconds to know what happened to an animal," Stone said. "It takes longer to prove it." It's easy to guess the weapon in some cases. Bullet holes and pellet shot left in the body tell Stone what kind and caliber of firearm was used. It can also tell him how far away the hunter was, whether the birds were resting or in flight, and even the position of many birds in a group. Stone and his staff perform blood tests, tissue analysis, and necropsies (autopsies) before they make a diagnosis.

Some cases are not as straightforward as a gunshot, however. For example, if a hawk is found dead on the side of the road, with several broken bones, it may appear to have been hit by a car. But that's not enough for Stone. He looks deeper to see if there are any other factors at work. Perhaps the raptor was diseased or poisoned, becoming disoriented and unable to fly properly. A sick or confused hawk wouldn't be able to get out of the way of a car. As pathologists dig deeper into how animals die, they also uncover how the everyday activities of humans can harm the environment.

GET THE LEAD OUT

The use of lead in paints and many other products has been proven dangerous to people and wildlife who swallow it. As birds feed they pick up pellets on shooting ranges, or swallow the lead sinkers lost in the water by fishermen. Ward Stone found as many as 40 percent of dead waterfowl in New York State died from swallowing lead sinkers.

Each of the 15,000 shooting ranges in the United States contains thousands of pellets. Stone examined one goose that had more than 400 lead pellets in its gizzard at the time it died.

In England, so many mute swans were killed by lead poisoning that lead shot and sinkers were banned. Stone is working for a similar ban in the United States. In the meantime, Stone tells fishermen that they can save lives by using sinkers made of steel or bismuth, which are as easily found in stores as lead ones.

PESTICIDE POISONING

In late May 1996, a homeowner in New York State treated his lawn to kill grubs. Later in the day he looked out the window and found a flock of thirty-one Canada geese dead in his yard. In another part of the state a man noticed several dead geese in his neighborhood.

These ducks were killed by Diazinon on grain . . .

. . . and these geese were killed by Diazinon on a golf course lawn.

The Case of the Disappearing Peregrine

In the 1960s peregrine falcons along with brown pelicans, ospreys, and eagles were becoming less common. Concerned scientists believed that somehow pesticides were the cause, although birds that were tested contained fairly low levels of the pesticides in their bodies. It was not until one British scientist, Derek Ratcliffe, noticed that the eggs of affected birds were unusually fragile and lightweight that the mystery became clear. As DDT broke down in the soil it produced a compound called DDE. The DDE accumulated in the bodies of worms, insects, and other animals, moving up the food chain in increasing concentrations. The high levels of DDE in birds caused them to produce and lay thin-shelled eggs that broke under the weight of the adult bird during incubation. Ratcliffe measured eggs in museums and found that eggs collected after 1947 weighed less and were thinner than those collected before 1947. The mystery was solved. The widespread use of DDT and similar pesticides began in 1947. It wasn't until 1972 that the use of DDT was banned in the United States.

Even so, North American birds are still exposed to DDT when they migrate to countries in South and Central America, where the pesticide is still used. Conservationists continue to work globally toward a ban of the production and use of these pesticides.

Later that same year, six mallards were found dead after eating cracked corn on a chemically treated lawn. The death toll mounts. These and other cases fill the Pathology Unit's yearly reports. For more than thirty years, Stone has been detecting and documenting thousands of cases of poisoned pigeons and dead ducks, and has built a wall of evidence against the use of many pesticides, including one called Diazinon. A chemical related to World War II nerve gas, Diazinon has been widely used since 1954. Long thought to break down quickly in the soil, it is now known to last for weeks. Homeowners spread it on their gardens and lawns to get rid of aphids, grubs, and other insects. But it is also absorbed by earthworms that are then eaten by songbirds. Granules of the chemical are picked up by grazing birds such as ducks and geese. Birds poisoned with Diazinon suffer violent convulsions and a horrible death.

How do we stop the killing? Stone says, by educating the public and calling for a ban on the use of these chemicals. In 1987, Stone testified against the use of Diazinon in a historic hearing that

Peregrine Falcon (*Falco peregrinus*)

The peregrine falcon is one of the fastest birds in the world, reaching speeds of up to 200 miles (320 kilometers) per hour as it dives to catch its prey in midair. Falcons primarily feed on other birds such as songbirds and waterfowl. This medium-size hawk normally nests on cliff ledges in mountainous areas, but has adapted well to life in big cities, nesting on window ledges and the balconies of tall buildings. In 1975 there were only 324 nesting pairs in the United States, but captive breeding programs, protecting nest sites, and the ban of DDT have helped the falcons recover to more than 1,600 pairs in 1998. They have recovered so successfully that the peregrine falcon is set to be "delisted," or taken off, the endangered species list.

resulted in a partial ban on the product. Diazinon can no longer be used on sod farms and golf courses, two places that attract large bird populations. Unfortunately the chemical can still be used by homeowners and easily bought in hardware stores and supermarkets. Stone continues to work toward a complete ban on its use in the United States just as DDT was banned in 1972.

But even a banned chemical can still kill. Pesticides are invisible killers that accumulate unnoticed in the soil. Some poisons, such as DDT, which has been banned for almost thirty years, and others that have been banned for more than ten years are still lurking in the environment and killing birds and other animals today.

Every year when new pesticides come on the market, wildlife pathologists brace themselves for the possibility of more mysterious deaths. New chemicals mean more detective work and new diagnostic tests to uncover the killers.

5 IT'S IN THE GENES

Mosquitoes may make us itch when they bite, but they can be deadly to birds. Mosquitoes carry a disease called malaria that has plagued mammals and birds for thousands of years. But only in the last two hundred years has the disease attacked native birds on the islands of Hawaii. There is evidence that the first mosquitoes hitched a ride to the islands on a whaling ship in 1826, and since then many species of Hawaiian birds have disappeared. Half of the native bird species are now extinct, and nearly half of those that remain are endangered. It's not all the fault of mosquitoes, of course. There are many reasons—loss of habitat, competition from nonnative birds and rats—but scientists believe that one of the major culprits is avian (bird) malaria.

Although malaria was suspected, biologists didn't fully understand how it continued in a population of rare and isolated birds, until they discovered that the malaria was present in alien birds, about fifteen species of birds brought to the islands from Asia, Africa, and the Americas. These birds carry the disease, but do not get sick. The mosquitoes, like little malaria-injection machines, bite the infected carriers and move the parasite to native birds that have no resistance to the deadly disease.

While testing the blood samples of 311 wild native birds, Dr. Rebecca Cann, an evolutionary geneticist at the University of Hawaii, found that a small population of 41 native birds called amakihi, on the Hawaiian island of Oahu, did not have malaria. Why?

"The only birds that can survive may be the ones that have inherited a certain set of genes that allows them to tolerate the disease," said Dr. Cann. These genes may act like an internal vaccine. As a geneticist, Dr. Cann studies heredity, how traits are passed down from generation to generation, and how certain traits, like not getting sick from malaria, evolve.

Dr. Rebecca Cann gets a close look at a color-banded i'iwi.

DNA

Inside every living cell is the blueprint of life—genetic material called DNA (deoxyribonucleic acid). DNA contains instructions for how an organism is made. It controls the length of an ostrich's legs, the color of a peacock's tail, and the speed of a hummingbird's wings. An animal gets one half of its DNA from its mother and one half from its father. DNA is coiled up in the cell's nucleus in threadlike strands called chromosomes. Sections of the chromosomes are called genes. By studying the genes and DNA, scientists can help endangered species reproduce, and discover ways to prevent and cure diseases.

"What we're doing is trying to compare different genetic sequences, the arrangement of DNA, in these amakihi to other birds from different places on the island that don't seem to have the resistance," Dr. Cann said.

From a tiny sample of blood, Dr. Cann extracts DNA and uses a process called polymerase chain reaction (PCR) to create multiple copies of the genetic material. She and her colleagues are looking for a genetic marker, a pattern of DNA that is unique and easily identifiable. The scientists use these markers to see whether similar and appropriate genes exist in other birds.

"The population I'm studying right now, [the amakihi] is not endangered, but it is closely related to other species that are endangered, critically endangered," Dr. Cann said. She feels that if they can find the gene or genes in the nonendangered amakihi that help it resist or tolerate the disease, then they will find important clues for locating those genes in more endangered birds.

If what they hope to find is true, and there is a gene that protects against malaria, then biologists can someday screen birds for the beneficial gene and use those individuals in captive rearing programs to artificially boost the species immunity. In this way, they may be able to produce a whole generation of disease-resistant birds that can be released back into the wild.

FAMILY TIES

Several years ago, when a team of Hawaiian researchers were capturing birds for a captive breeding program, they hoped they had an even number of males and females, but they weren't sure. With some birds, it's difficult, almost impossible to tell the difference between the male and female of a species. Scientists would have to rely on the one major clue—who laid the eggs. The only other way to tell the sex of some birds is by performing a surgical procedure to identify the reproductive organs, something biologists obviously can't do in the field.

But now, with just a tiny drop of blood or a few feathers, lab technicians can tell the gender of the bird by looking at its DNA fingerprint, a map of the bird's genetic material. They can also tell who its parents are and who its closest relatives are. This is important when zoos and wildlife centers are trying to breed birds and

Arlene Kumamoto, a cryogenetics scientist at CRES frozen ZOO, part of the San Diego Zoo, selects a specimen of genetic material.

maintain a wide variety of genetic material in order to preserve the species.

All the genes represented in a group of animals is called the gene pool, and scientists believe that a healthy population has a wide range of different genes. This is called genetic diversity. When only a few individuals of a species are left, the size of the gene pool is smaller, and new offspring may be more vulnerable to genetic disease. To produce the healthiest offspring possible, scientist breed only those animals that are as distantly related as possible. Someday scientists may even be able to produce whole flocks of birds from the genetic material of rare or extinct species.

6 RARE EGGS

In 1960 biologists discovered that there were only 15 whooping cranes left in the world. In 1985 only six California condors remained in the wild, and in 1996, fewer than one hundred small birds called puaiohi were left in the forests of Hawaii. Fortunately for the birds and us, these numbers have increased, thanks to the hard work of biologists who wouldn't give up. But how do you rescue a species that is so close to extinction? By creating more birds.

The breeding of animals in zoos and wildlife centers is called captive breeding and involves mating unrelated males and females of a species. It sounds simple, but is far from it when the fate of an entire species is at stake. The goal is to re-create as close as possible the key elements in the habitat that promote mating and successful rearing of the young. Some birds need specific cues to let them know it's time to mate, like rainfall or a change in light. There are hundreds of captive breeding

A delicate Hawaiian puaiohi

programs going on all over the world, and each one is different, designed specifically for a particular species. But one of the most dramatic rescues involves the California condor.

CAPTIVE CONDORS

More than a hundred years ago, large scavenging birds called condors soared over much of the western United States. But their numbers declined as settlers hunted large herd animals. Condors fed on the carcasses and were shot as pests. Settlers also made a hobby of collecting condor eggs. The condor's wide-open habitat was changed to farms and communities. By the 1970s only a small group of condors remained in the mountains of Southern California.

In a historic attempt to rescue the species from certain extinction, the condors were collected and taken to the San Diego Wild Animal Park. The last wild condor was captured in 1987. The plan was to increase the condor population enough to release young birds back into the wild.

Successfully hand rearing an endangered species is extremely difficult when almost nothing is known about them. How warm do you keep the eggs? How long is incubation? What will the hatchlings eat? It's often a case of trial and error, experimenting with diets and temperatures until they get it right. Scientists commonly use a surrogate species to develop basic techniques for taking care of an endangered animal. The surrogate species is usually not endangered, but not always. If it weren't for the work done on the rare Andean condor there wouldn't be any California condors left. Scientists learned everything from getting the right temperature and humidity for incubating condor eggs to the feeding and care of newborns.

It's important to keep the chicks well fed, and to make sure they imprint on other condors. Imprinting is how a condor chick learns that it is a condor. In the wild, a young bird imprints on the first moving thing it sees, usually its parent. It watches and learns all it needs to know. But in captivity young birds, especially ducks and geese, have been known to imprint on humans. Biologists must stay out of sight and let the young imprint on other condors so they will be able to find a mate in the wild. Biologists use a condor look-alike puppet to feed the chicks their bits of meat, and keep out of view behind a screen or curtain.

When the condors are old enough, they are moved to a large outdoor flight pen, where they stay for several months before they are released. Even after release, the condors are not completely on their own. Biologists leave food out for the scavengers so they won't starve or eat contaminated food.

By 1998, there were 49 California condors in the wild, but it's still an uphill battle. The same problems the wild condors faced prior to captive breeding still exist. Several condors have died from lead poisoning, colliding with power lines, and eating contaminat-

California Condor (*Gymnogyps californianus*)

The California condor is the largest flying bird in North America. It has a wingspan of 9 feet (2.7 meters) and is so heavy it sometimes has difficulty getting off the ground. Condors are scavengers and need to soar over vast expanses of open country to search for dead animal carcasses. Condors begin breeding when they are six years old, and then lay only one egg every other year. The California Condor Recovery Program plans to build up two wild populations, in California and Arizona, with 150 birds in each by the year 2020.

ed carcasses that ranchers leave out for coyotes. One condor died from contact with automobile antifreeze.

To prevent these large birds from colliding with power lines, the Condor Recovery Program started a new kind of training for them. Scientists set up power-line poles wired with low-voltage cables inside the condor cages. Every time a condor lands on a pole they receive a slight shock. Biologists also taught the condors to stay away from humans by sneaking up behind a bird, picking it up, and flipping it onto its back. So far several trained condors have been released and have successfully avoided power lines, people, and other hazards.

RESCUING HAWAII'S BIRDS

Breeding one of the largest birds in the world, the condor, is difficult enough, but how do you raise one of the smallest? That's what concerned the breeding specialists at the Peregrine Fund's Keauhou Bird Conservation Center in Hawaii, where scientists are breeding some of the rarest birds in the world.

A brightly colored male akepa

"What we do is collect eggs from birds in the wild, and artificially incubate, and hand rear the chicks either for release, or for captive propagation," said Joseph Kuhn, a biologist with the Peregrine Fund. They have developed the techniques required to successfully hatch and raise eleven species of Hawaiian birds, and the smallest, so far, is the tiny akepa, a type of honeycreeper found only in Hawaii.

Field biologists with the U.S. Fish and Wildlife Service and the U.S. Geological Survey found two akepa eggs inside a hole in a tree

Joseph Kuhn and Tom Snetsinger at work in the Hawaiian rain forest

branch 30 feet (9 meters) above the ground during a routine search of the forest. Only an ornithologist with a keen eye could have found them because the eggs are the size of a little round peanut. The akepa eggs were placed in a thermos full of warmed millet, lowered down to a mobile egg brooder, and rushed back to the Conservation Center.

Taking eggs from wild nests early in the season is called double-clutching. "Borrowing" the first clutch of eggs causes the female to lay and raise a second clutch. It's one way to double the number of eggs a pair lays in a season.

On June 23, 1998, only one chick hatched. Feeding time was tricky. It took a steady hand and a sharp eye to get the bits of bee larvae into the tiny, wobbly mouth. The first akepa ever born in captivity may eventually get a mate, but it could take some time. "It's a small green bird in a big green forest," Kuhn said. It'll be dif-

NASA in the Nest

How do scientists know how warm to keep bald eagle eggs? They use some of the most sophisticated equipment in outer space—an infrared thermal imaging video camera developed by NASA. This camera "sees" heat and can determine the precise temperature inside the incubating eggs. Knowing how warm the eggs are, scientists will be able to develop a better incubator that will improve the survival of endangered birds.

Alala (*Corvus hawaiiensis*)

The Hawaiian crow looks like other crows in the United States, large and glossy black, but unlike other crows the alala is a highly specialized bird that has adapted to the high-elevation rain forest on the big island of Hawaii. It eats mainly fruit, nectar, and insects. The alala isn't equipped to adapt to changes in its habitat, or defend itself against nonnative predators. Besides breeding the alala, conservationists are also ridding its habitat of cats and rats.

ficult to find more eggs. But in the meantime this team is working with other endangered species such as the puaiohi (small Kauai thrush) and alala (Hawaiian crow).

Many factors affect the success or failure of breeding: weather, malaria-carrying mosquitoes, predatory rats, and even meat-eating ants. During the first years of breeding the alala, all cords and wires had to be coated with Vaseline, and table legs placed in moats of water, to keep the ants from getting inside the incubators.

Although captive breeding of the alala is going well, its wild population is small. They are preyed upon by the Hawaiian hawk, and infected with a bacteria that is spread by feral (wild) cats. As of 1998, there were thirty-one alala, twenty-two in captivity and nine living in the wild.

7 OPERATION MIGRATION

Breeding birds is just one step in rebuilding a species. The second step is returning them to the wild. Sometimes that means teaching birds new skills to deal with the dangers of living near people, as the Condor Recovery Program discovered, or how to adapt to a new home. Bald eagles and peregrine falcons are our success stories in reintroducing bird species to their original habitats. Once near extinction, both species have increased to such a high number that they have been "downlisted" from endangered to threatened.

Like the bird-breeding programs, successful reintroduction works well when scientists simulate the species' chick-rearing techniques. For example, in New York State bald eagles are reintroduced using a process called "hacking." Seven- to eight-week-old chicks were placed in an artificial nest at the top of a 35-foot (11-meter) hack tower. Biologists brought food to the young until the eaglets were old enough to fend for themselves. From inside the nest, the birds learned the landscape. After their winter migration, the eagles usually returned to the same area to mate and raise their young.

Hack towers are fine for eagles, but puffins don't like heights. These oceangoing birds raise their chicks in underground nests. When Dr. Stephen Kress reintroduced puffins to an island in Maine, he had to construct burrows. A chick was placed inside each nest, and biologists brought food to it every day. After three weeks, the puffin chicks came out of their holes. They too imprinted on the landscape, and today there are several successful puffin nesting colonies in Maine.

For some species, however, it's not enough to just leave the birds and hope they return. Birds such as cranes, geese, ducks, and swans must be taught how to go home.

SHOW ME THE WAY TO GO HOME

Two hundred years ago more than 100,000 trumpeter swans traveled the Eastern Seaboard. Trumpeters are the largest waterbirds in the world, weighing in at 30 pounds (12 kilograms), but their size and beauty have often proved fatal. Early settlers hunted the graceful white birds to near extinction for their eggs and meat. The feathers were used as powder puffs, quill pens, and as decorations on ladies' hats. By the 1930s, no trumpeters existed in the East.

But they may be coming back, thanks to scientists who are willing to be swan-moms and tour guides. Scientists from the Environmental Studies Center at Airlie in Virginia are teaching trumpeter swans how to migrate from western New York to Maryland.

Putting the swans back into western New York is not just an interesting experiment; it's important for the environment. Another type of swan has moved into the trumpeters' habitat with disastrous results. Mute swans are native to Europe, but were brought to this country more than a hundred years ago and released on large estates and in city parks. Some mute swans escaped to the wild, where they adapted and reproduced. Now, biologists are finding that wild mute swans are disrupting the natural balance of an ecosystem. They are aggressive predators that drive off smaller nesting birds and destroy their eggs. They upset wetland ecology by eating 4 to 8 pounds (2 to 3.5 kilograms) of plants per day, roots and all. Trumpeter swans have evolved as part

You can tell a trumpeter swan by its black bill. Mute swans have an orange bill.

A trumpeter swan flying with Gavin Shire's ultralight plane

of these ecosystems and do not have the same disastrous effect. The hope is that reintroducing trumpeter swans will keep mute swans from taking over.

To get the trumpeters back where they belong, they will be taught how to migrate using the method pioneered by Canadian Bill Lishman and made famous in the movie *Fly Away Home*.

"The ability to fly is instinctual," said Gavin Shire, lead biologist for the Migratory Bird Project, "but to migrate has to be taught." Unlike songbirds, which are born knowing how and when to travel to warmer climates in the fall, swans, cranes, and geese learn the way home from their parents.

The lessons start before birth. "We played the sounds of the ultralight aircraft while the eggs were still in the incubators," Shire said. When the chicks hatched they imprinted on the biologists, who became swan-moms. Unlike condors or cranes, swans learn that they are swans from the rest of the flock and won't have trouble finding a mate.

Flying lessons started on the ground as the chicks waddled after the plane as it rolled slowly along the grass. Eventually the chicks followed it into the air. These test runs taught the swans to follow the plane and become familiar with the landscape. "They will hopefully imprint on the area, so it becomes their biological compass," Shire said.

Some swans learned faster than others, but soon most of them learned to take up position at either side of the plane's wingtips, creating a short V as Shire shouted encouragement.

But not everything always goes as planned. On December 4, 1998, two pilots and eighteen trained swans took off at dawn headed south. The flight went smoothly until their first landing. As the plane slowed down, the birds came too close to the engine. One bird caught a leg in the ultralight's propeller. A second bird wounded its wing a day later.

Scientists learn to be flexible when problems occur, and Shire and his team quickly developed an alternative plan. They trucked the birds along the migration route, taking them out every 35 miles (56 kilometers) or so to fly the swans in a 5- or 6- mile (8- to 9.5 kilometer) radius. This allowed the swans to learn the landscape in sections. The birds spent the winter in Maryland, but there was concern as to whether the flock would return north the following spring. It didn't.

Most of the swans remained south, but one was unaccounted for. It was finally spotted near Rochester, New York. For one swan, at least, the experiment was a success. In any experiment even failures are valuable, because they teach scientists how to improve their methods for the future.

Canada geese and sandhill cranes have also been taught to migrate, and each flight has taught scientists more about this complex process so that eventually it can be used to help endangered species. In 1997 pilot Kent Clegg flew, for the first time, four endangered whooping cranes along with a small band of sandhill cranes from Grace, Idaho, to Bosque del Apache National Wildlife Refuge, New Mexico. The experimental migration route chosen by Clegg held many dangers. Whooping cranes are such large birds that they tend to soar on thermal currents. But on this trip they had to constantly flap their wings. Whoopers fell out of the sky exhausted. The route also took the birds through eagle territory, where one crane was attacked by a golden eagle.

Training whooping cranes is an international endeavor involving Canadian and U.S. wildlife officials because the only migratory flock travels more than 2,500 miles (4,000 kilometers) between Canada and Texas. A second migratory flock in the East will ensure that the cranes will not disappear from the wild if pollution, hurricanes, or disease were to wipe out the Texas flock. Before a new migrating population can be formed, however, both governments must agree on where the habitats will lie and who will monitor and protect the birds.

Whooping Cranes (*Grus americanus*)

The whooping crane is the tallest bird in North America standing up to 5 feet (1.5 meters). Adult cranes are snow white with black wing tips and a red forehead. They live in grassy wetlands where they feed on small animals such as crayfish and other crustaceans, insects, fish, frogs, and plants. In 1941 there were only 15 whooping cranes recorded. Captive breeding programs boosted the crane population to 375 by 1998. The only migratory flock consists of 180 birds that fly between Wood Buffalo National Park in Canada and the Aransas National Wildlife Refuge in Texas. Other nonmigratory flocks exist in Florida and in breeding centers in Maryland, Wisconsin, and Calgary, Canada.

8 PROTECTING EARTH AND SKY

A habitat is a home. When we change the landscape to fit our needs, we're changing and destroying another species' home. So far more than one half of all wetlands in the United States have been drained or filled, and only 1 percent of the tallgrass prairies in the Midwest remain. Altering the environment continues every day, but so do the efforts of many scientists and citizens who are trying to stop the devastating effects our actions have on other species.

The study of how animals and humans interact with each other and the environment is called ecology. Ecologists and other scientists spend much of their time learning about these interactions and trying to make them better. Identifying and preserving important habitats is a top priority. An important habitat is often a place that has a high level of biodiversity, meaning it has many different kinds of animals and plants.

One way ecologists identify high biodiversity areas is by using a complex computer model called Geographic Information Systems (GIS), which analyzes information from many different sources— road maps, telemetry studies, migration routes, and plant distribution. By layering distribution maps of everything from ants to eagles, ecologists can build a complete picture of an area's biodiversity and pinpoint land that should be protected. But birds can't be contained in a national park or controlled by boundaries. Their home is the sky, and it's not enough just to protect the land. People will have to limit the dangers that some human activities cause.

MIMICKING MOTHER NATURE

Ecologists in Florida learned that decades of draining water out of the Everglades for human use has made the area too dry even for snails to survive. That was bad news for the snail, and for a raptor called the snail kite whose favorite food is the apple snail. But when biologists raised the water level to help the kite, they created a second problem. The water was now too high for the wood stork, another bird that nests and feeds in the Everglades. Storks need shallow water during nesting time so they can catch large amounts of fish to feed their chicks. With the water too high, some storks were unable to raise their young.

The solution? Biologists have learned to mimic Mother Nature by artificially fluctuating the water level throughout the year. They make sure the water is deeper in some areas to benefit the snail, and shallow during the wood stork's nesting season. By creating a balance, both birds as well as hundreds of other animals and plants can survive.

Altering nature's course for our own purposes has backfired for other species. People have been preventing forest fires for centuries, not realizing that many species depend on occasional fires to reproduce. The jack pine is one tree that needs the heat from a forest fire to open its cones and spill its seeds onto the ashy ground.

Without fires, jack pines were disappearing, replaced by hardwood trees and red pines. No one thought much about this change

Kirtland's Warbler (*Dendroica kirtlandii*)

This small yellow-breasted songbird nests in a small area of Michigan and winters in the Bahamas. Each year during the first two weeks of June, biologists and volunteers survey the population by listening to birdsong. Only male warblers sing when they establish territories, using songs to attract mates and defend against rival males. The songs can be heard from a quarter mile away and can be counted without disturbing the birds. In 1998, 805 singing males were recorded.

until bird-watchers noticed that the Kirtland's warbler was also in decline. This songbird lives in a small area of Michigan, and it's choosy about where it nests, preferring the sandy soil under older jack pines.

A change in the forest affected another bird also—the cowbird, which likes a more open hardwood forest. It lays its eggs in the nests of Kirtland's warblers and other birds. The changing habitat favored the cowbirds, and the warblers declined.

Today wildlife managers mimic Mother Nature by setting controlled fires, called "prescribed burns," to encourage the jack pines to grow. The Kirtland's warblers are making a comeback. In 1998 there were more than four times as many singing male warblers recorded than ten years before.

HEALTHY HABITATS

The Kirtland's warbler project and the Everglades plan are just two examples of large-scale habitat restoration. But making environments bird-friendly again can be as complex as manipulating an entire state's water supply, or as easy as turning off the lights.

Bright lights from cities confuse thousands of birds migrating at night. Every year at least 100 million birds die colliding with skyscrapers. But several organizations such as FLAP (Fatal Light Awareness Program) and Captains of Conservation have persuaded building owners to turn off lights or use blinds during migration seasons.

Another simple yet effective project focuses on helping the homeless. Most people under the age of fifty have never seen an eastern bluebird, and that's because bluebird populations declined by as much as 90 percent in the early 1900s because there was nowhere to nest.

Bluebirds build their nests in tree cavities, preferring dead trees, or woodpecker-riddled fence posts. But as suburbs spread, dead trees were felled, and wooden fence posts were replaced by metal and wire. Bluebirds had to compete for the limited nest sites with more aggressive house sparrows and starlings. The bluebirds were losing the battle.

In 1978 the North American Bluebird Society was founded, and the nest-box project began. Bluebirds used man-made nest boxes to raise their young in, as long as they were built just for them. Since then, several thousand specially designed nest boxes have been built and installed by bird-watchers, homeowners, conservation clubs, and scout troops, and many miles of bluebird trails (a path lined with nest boxes) have been created. Now that it's easier to find a home, the bluebirds are coming back.

HOW YOU CAN HELP

The nicest part about bird conservation is that you can do it in your own backyard. Here are a few ways that you can help birds that live in and migrate through your neighborhood:

▌ Plant native plants, shrubs, and trees for birds to feed off and nest in.

▌ Establish bird feeders and keep them filled throughout winter.

▌ Find out what birds in your region (like the bluebird or barn owl) would benefit from a nest box, and make one.

▌ Ask your parents to use safe, natural pest control instead of toxic pesticides.

▌ Use lead-free sinkers when you fish.

▌ Support conservation organizations in your area.

▌ Join Project FeederWatch or other citizen science groups.

GLOSSARY

captive breeding — producing and rearing young animals in a zoo or wildlife center.

DNA — deoxyribonucleic acid, the molecule in cells that contains coded genetic information.

double-clutching — taking eggs from a nest to encourage the female to lay a second clutch of eggs.

ecology — the study of the relationship between animals, people, and the environment.

genetics — the science of heredity and the way living things vary.

habitat — the place where an animal lives in nature.

hacking — a process of raising and releasing birds; originally developed for falconry.

migration — the seasonal movement of birds from one habitat to another.

nest parasitism — laying eggs in another species' nest so that the other species' adult will raise the parasite's young.

ornithology — the scientific study of birds.

passerine — refers to perching songbirds.

pathology — the scientific study of disease and causes of death.

raptor — a bird of prey, including eagles, hawks, falcons, and owls.

telemetry — the use of radio devices and other technology to track and monitor animals.

FURTHER READING

For more information on birds and how scientists study them, look for these and other books.

Endangered Birds of North America by April Pulley Sayre (Twenty-First Century Books, 1997)

Father Goose by Bill Lishman (Crown Pub., 1996)

Hawk Highway in the Sky: Watching Raptor Migration by Caroline Arnold (Harcourt Brace, 1997)

In Good Hands by Stephen R. Swinburne (Sierra Club, 1998)

Check out these and other sites on the Internet for even more bird information.

Cornell Lab of Ornithology — http://www.Birdsource.cornell.edu
   Learn about Project FeederWatch and other citizen science programs.

National Audubon Society — www.audubon.org/audubon/
   View Audubon's WatchList and Kidscope.

Peregrine Fund — www.peregrinefund.org
   This site will introduce you to several conservation projects that the fund is involved in.

The Point Reyes Bird Observatory — www.prbo.org
   Keep up to date with the birding newsletter and read about conservation programs. Good links to other sites.

Wake Forest University's Albatross Project — www.wfu.edu/albatross
   Follow the flights of albatross that have been fitted with transmitters. Learn how and why they can fly such long distances.

INDEX